COMPUTERS
OUR LIFELINE

A

MANOJ PUBLICATIONS

COMPUTERS
Our Lifeline - A

Publisher :

MANOJ PUBLICATIONS

761, Main Road, Burari, Delhi-110084
Ph.   : 27611116, 27611349
Fax   : 27611546, Mob. : 9868112194
email   : info@manojpublications.com
Website : www. manojpublications.com

Showroom :

1583-84, Dariba Kalan, Chandni Chowk, Delhi-110006
Ph. : 23262174, 23268216
Mobile : 9818753569

ISBN : 978-81-310-1950-4

Concept:
Puneet Gupta
M.B.A. (William & Mary, U.S.A.)

Edited by:
Davinder Singh Minhas

PREFACE

Learning computers is a must in today's Machine Age. Each and every work is being done with the use of different machines in the form of computers, LEDs, washing machines, microwave ovens, electric tandoor, mobile phones and so on. The list is endless and each new day dawns with a new invention, another new machine. So, it becomes imperative for every child to be familiar with the working knowledge of computers. There is no denying the fact that a little knowledge of computers makes our work easier and faster.

In this fast-paced life where computers have made their presence felt in every nook and corner of the world, a child's sound knowledge of computers stands him in good stead in the long run.

The present book is meant for the tiny tots who have just entered into the world of learning. Apart from the knowledge of other subjects, their familiarity with the concepts of computers at their tender age goes a long way in making them computer literates.

The book has been designed beautifully, keeping in mind the age-group at every stage of the book. We are more than sure that the book will come up to the expectations of the teacher and the taught. We shall be very much glad to entertain any constructive suggestion.

–Publisher

Contents

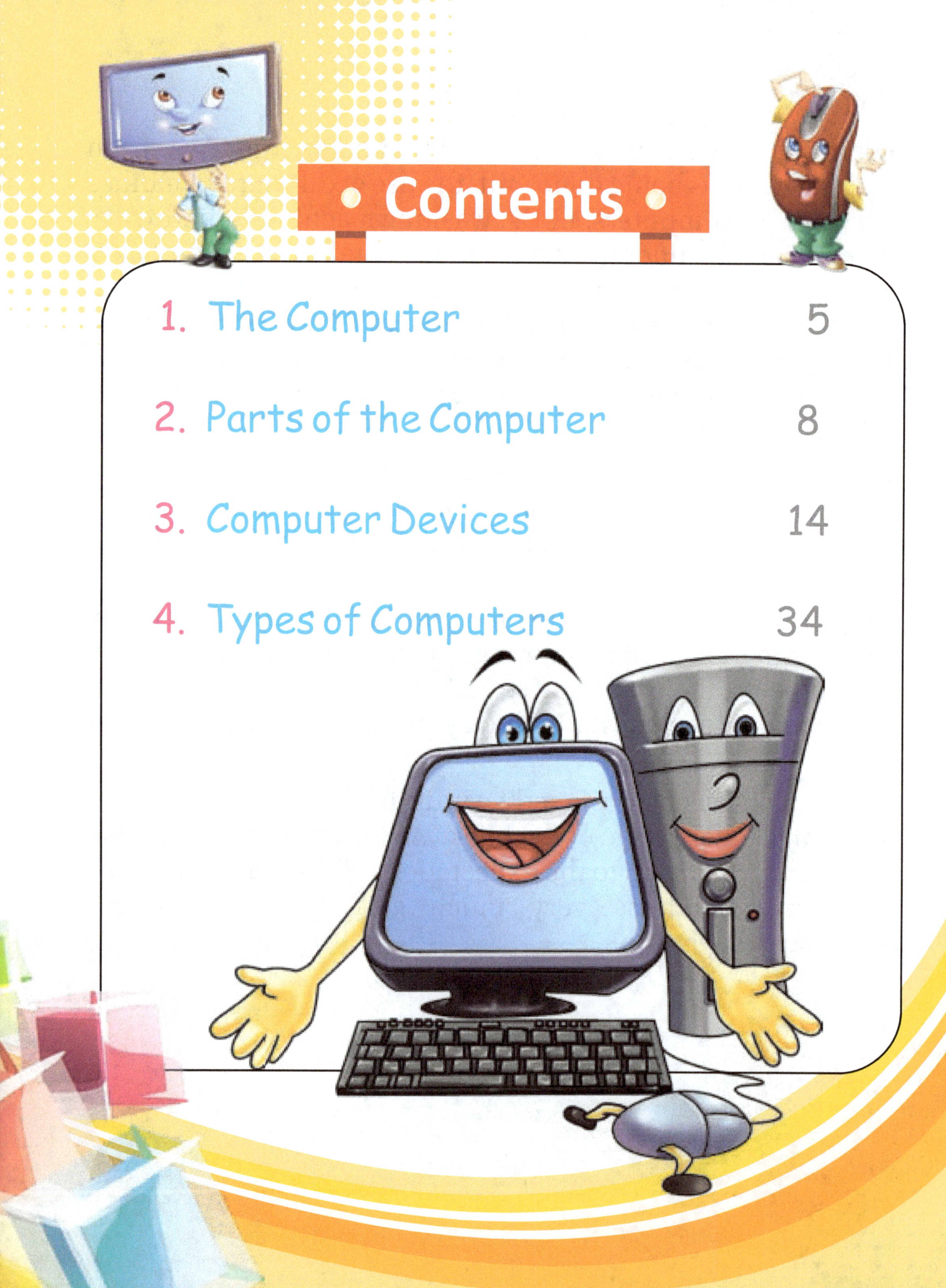

1 THE COMPUTER

I am a
Computer.

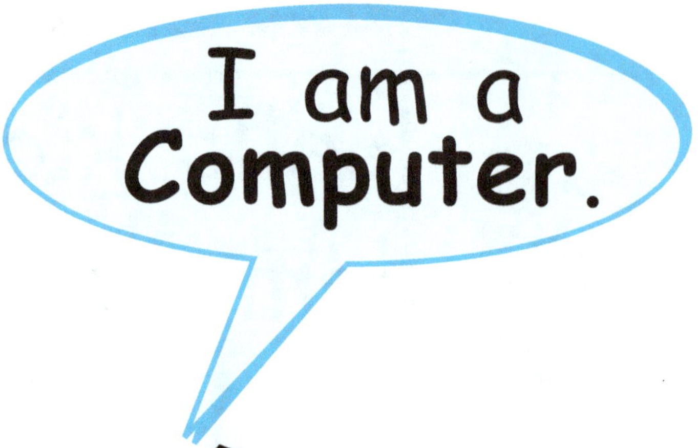

Please make
me colourful.

The Mouse, the Monitor, the Keyboard and the CPU are the parts of the computer.

This is a **Mouse.**

Please make me colourful.

This is a
Monitor.

Please make
me colourful.

Colour me.

Colour me.

The computer devices are attached to the computer.

This is a **Printer**.

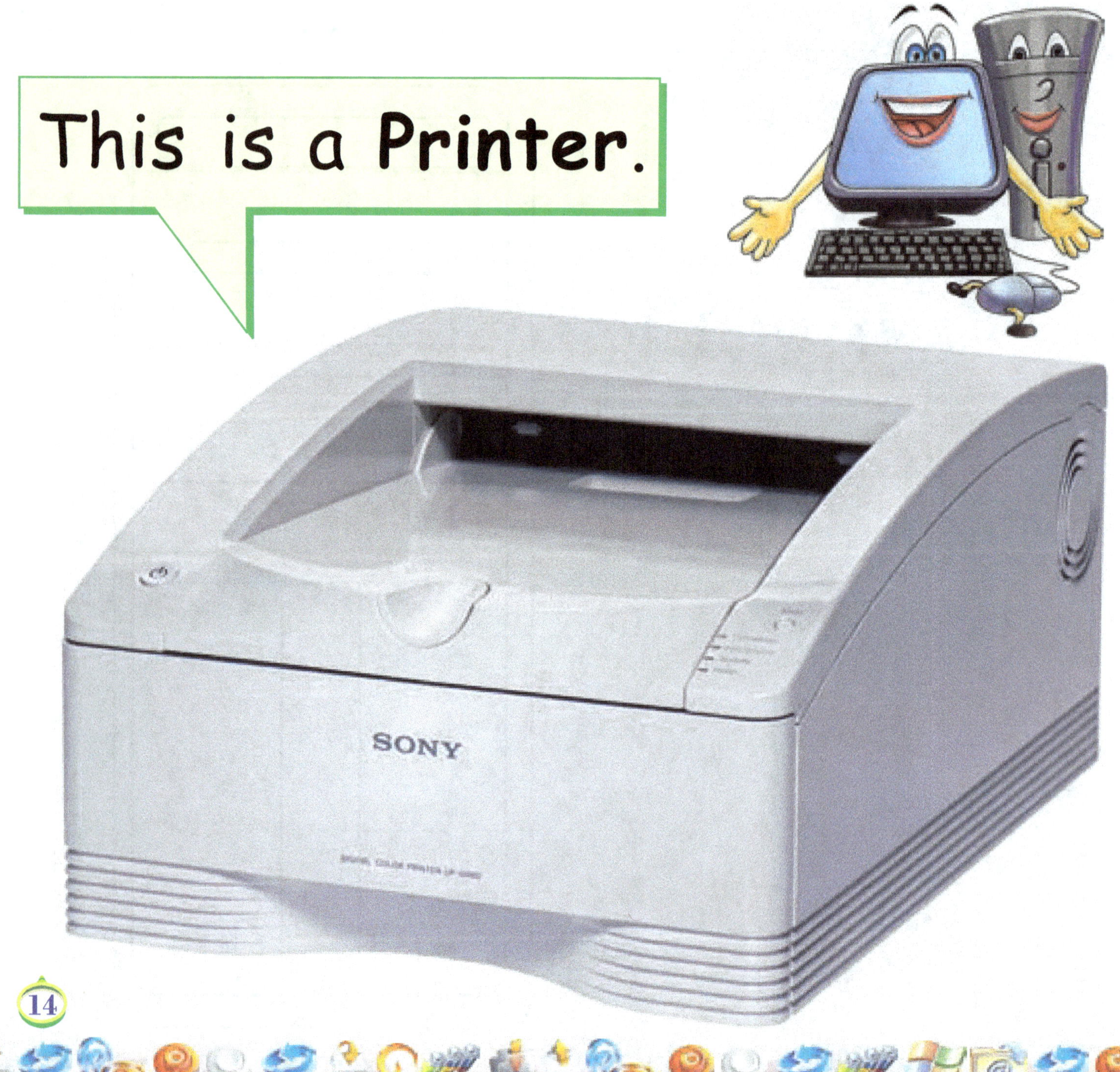

Please make me colourful.

This is a
Scanner.

Please make me colourful.

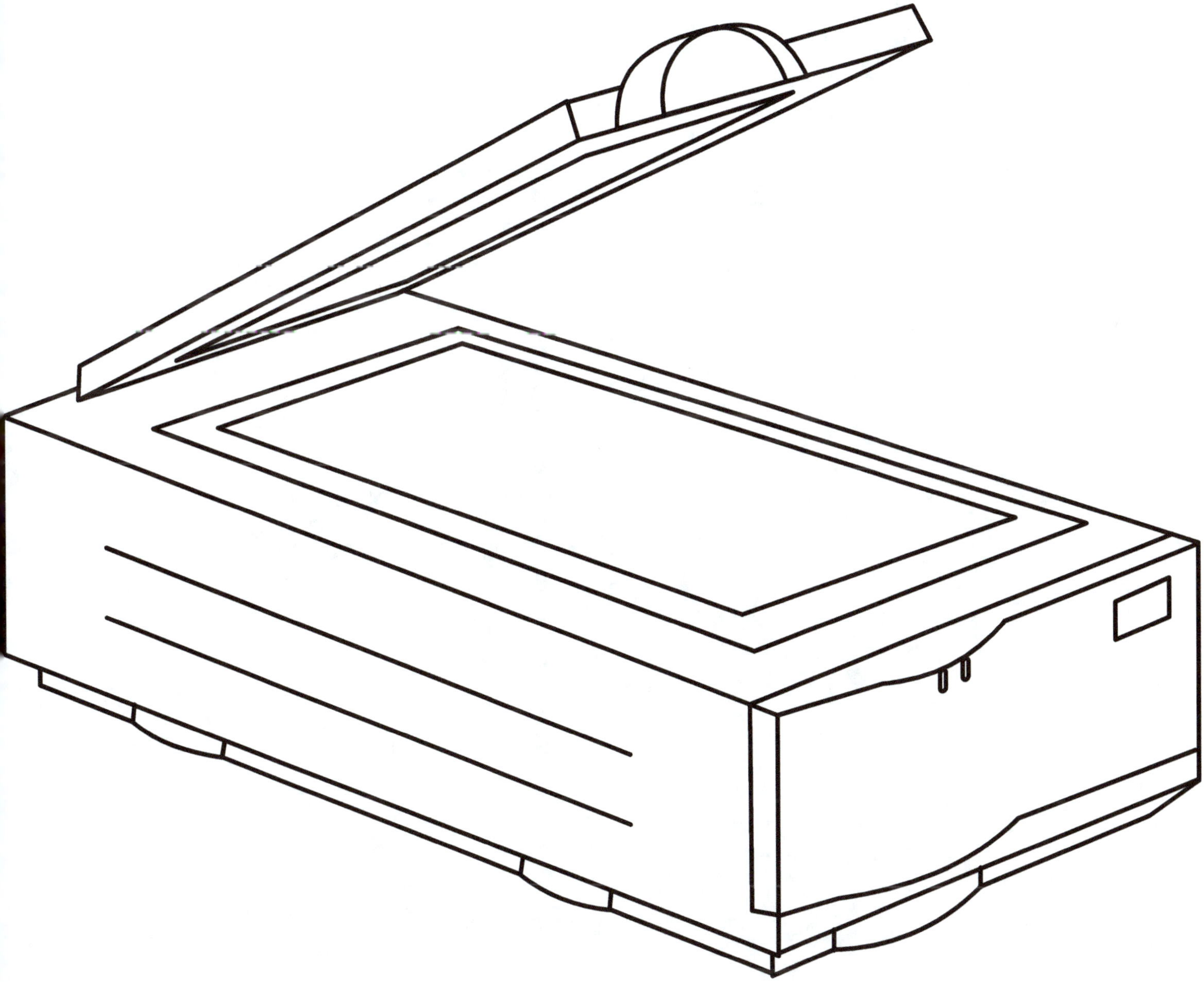

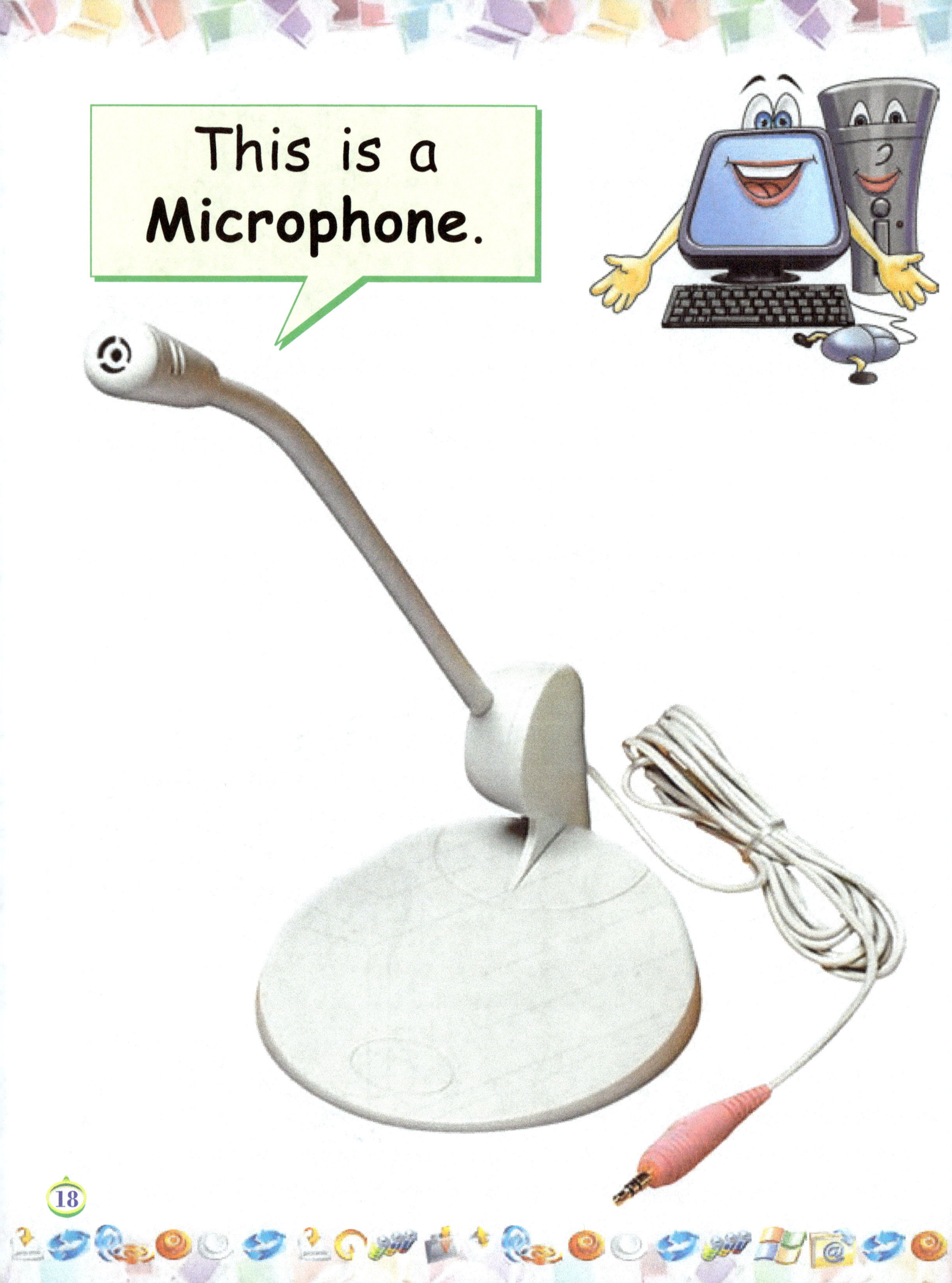

This is a
Microphone.

Please make
me colourful.

These are
Speakers.

Labtec
Labtec

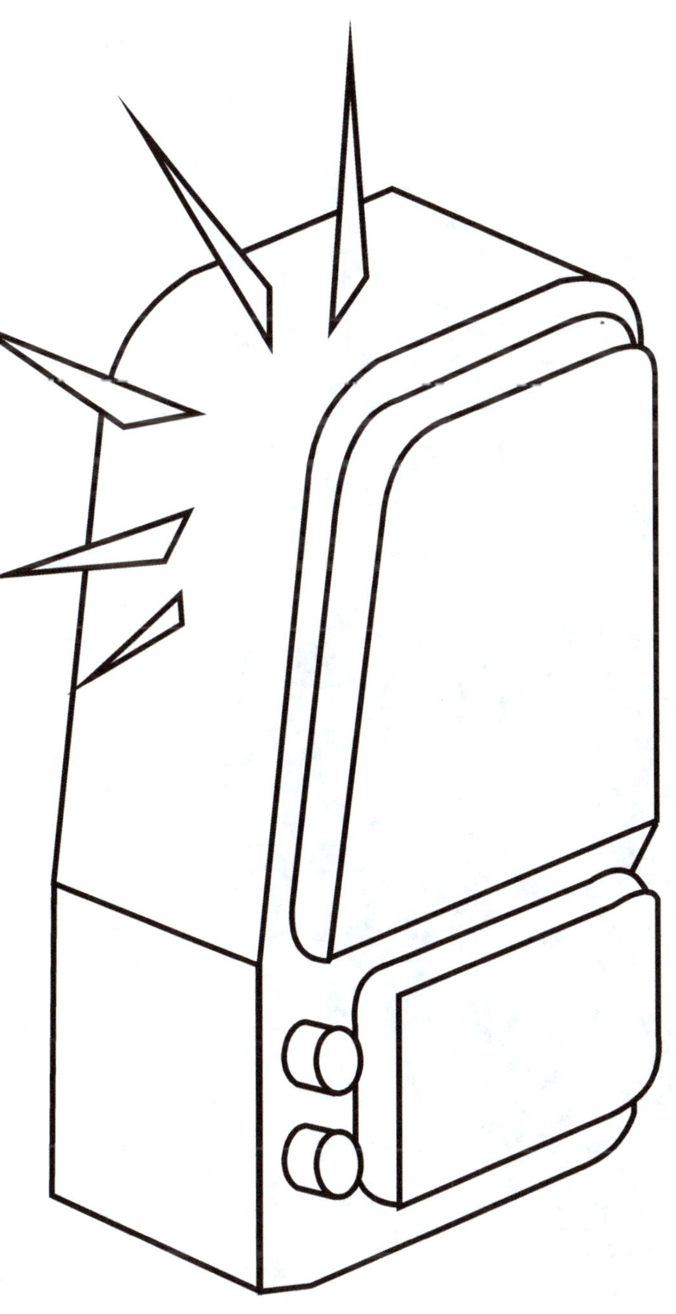

Please make us colourful.

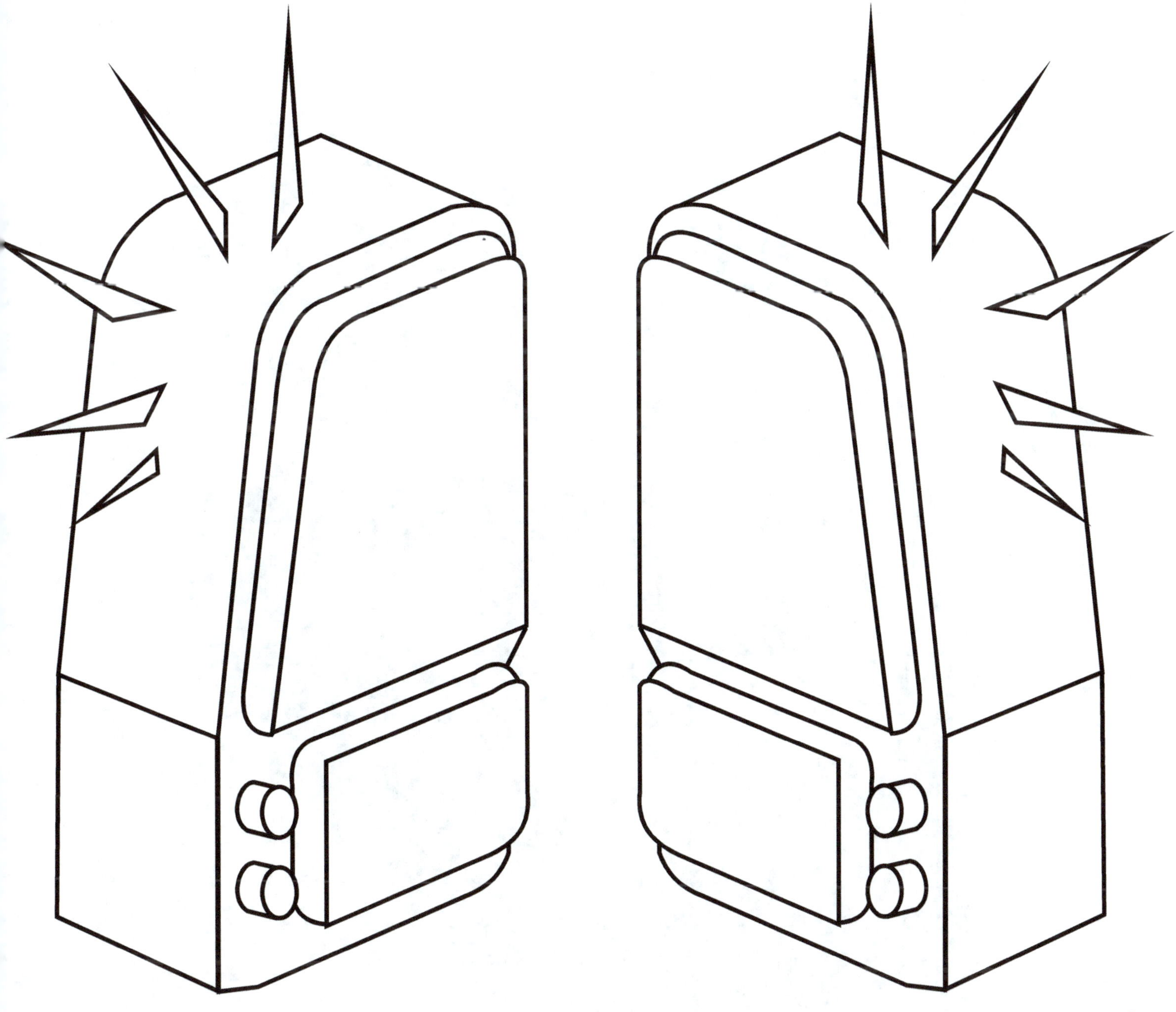

This is a UPS.

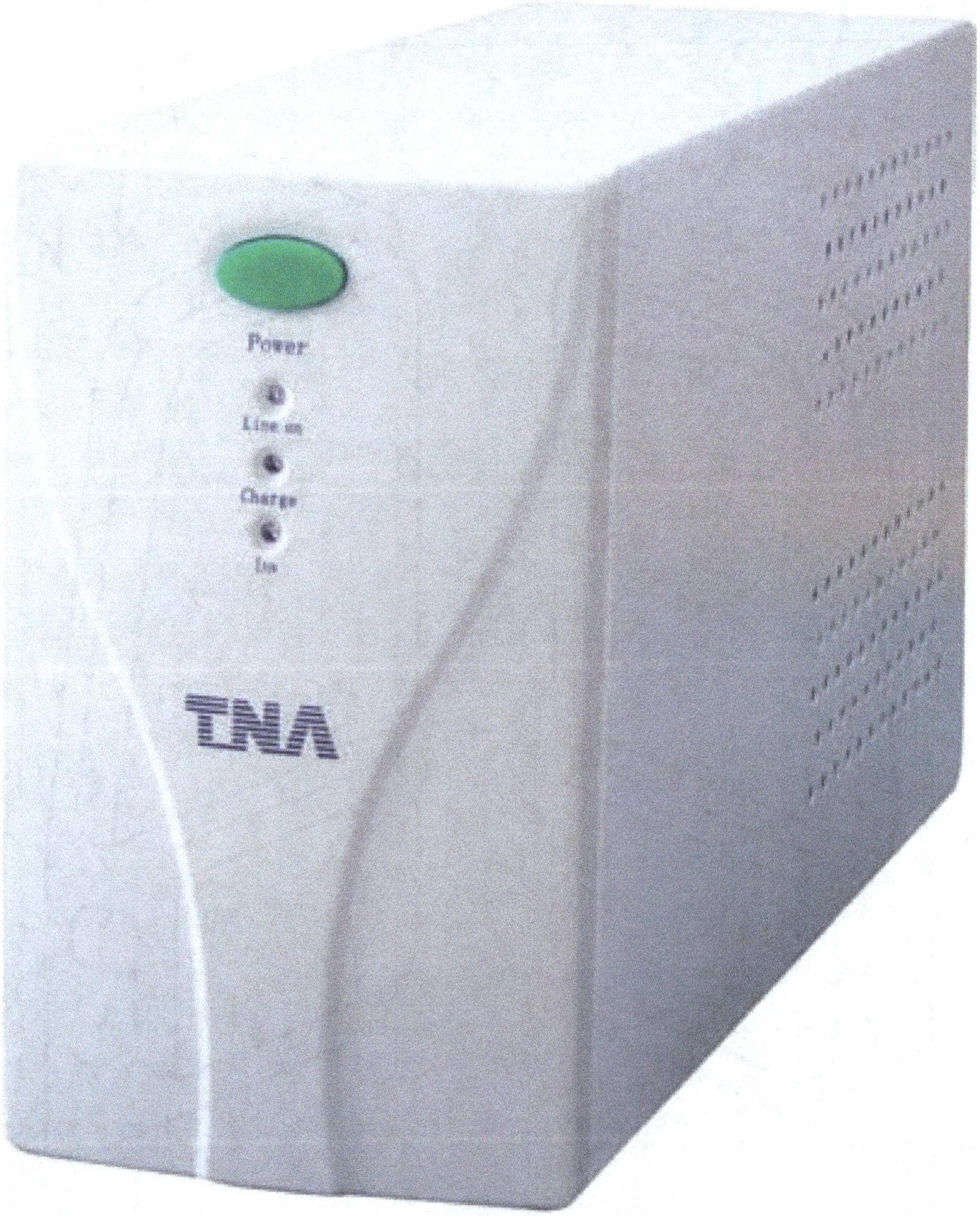

Power
Line on
Charge
In
TNA

Please make me colourful.

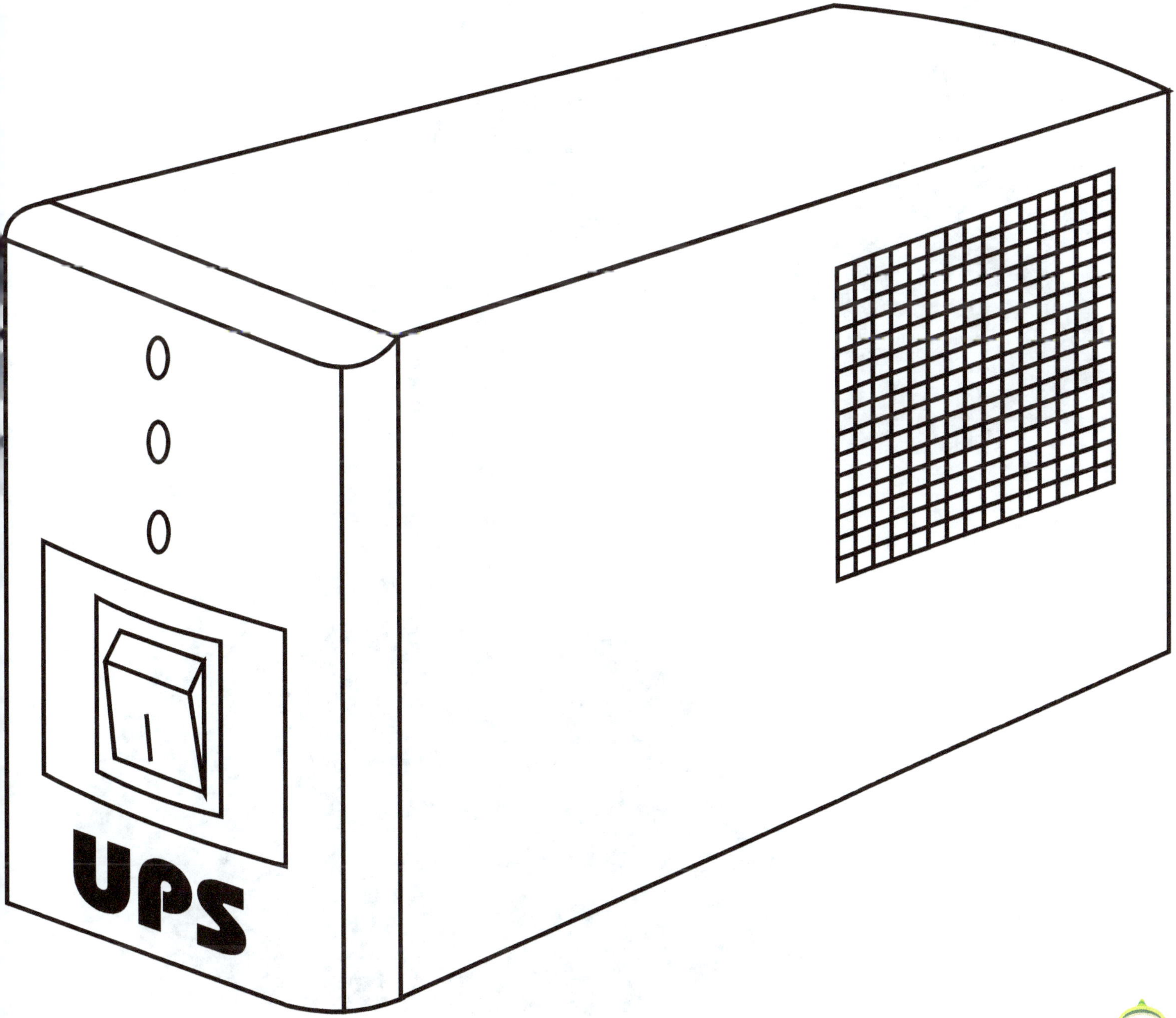

This is a
Joystick.
Genius

Please make
me colourful.

This is a
Floppy Disc.

MicroFLOPPY
Double Sided
1.44 MB

Please make me colourful.

MicroFLOPPY
Double Sided
1.44 MB

This is a
Compact Disc.

Please make me colourful.

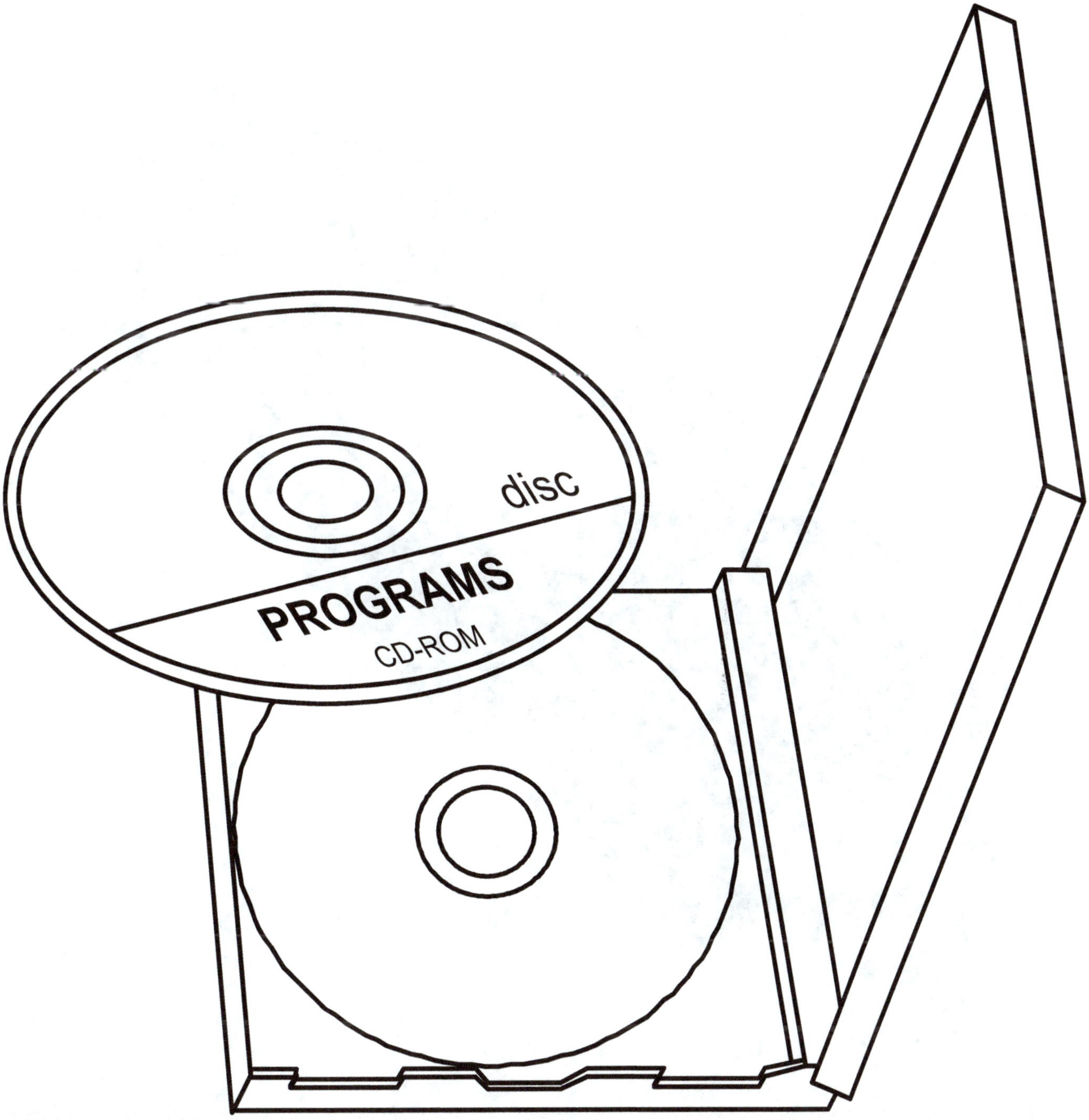

This is a
Pen Drive.

micro
2.0 GB
cruzer

Please make me colourful.

Find and circle the hidden computer parts.

Which computer is the bigger? Put a tick (✓) in the appropriate box.

This is a **Laptop**.

Please make me colourful.

This is a
Smartphone.

Start
Wednesday
September 05, 2007
11:59 AM
100%
19.11MB
75.45MB
iPAQ Wireless
Outlook E-mail: 7 Unread
Review Proposal
12:00PM-1:00PM (Dave's office)
1 Active task
1 High priority
Device unlocked
hp
Calendar
Contacts
iPAQ

Please make me colourful.
Google
Apps

This is a Tablet.

Please make
me colourful.

Look at the following pictures.

Now tell which of these is the same as shown in the picture above. Put a tick (✓) in the appropriate box.

www.ingramcontent.com/pod-product-compliance
Lightning Source LLC
Chambersburg PA
CBHW081304130726
47998CB00010B/2921